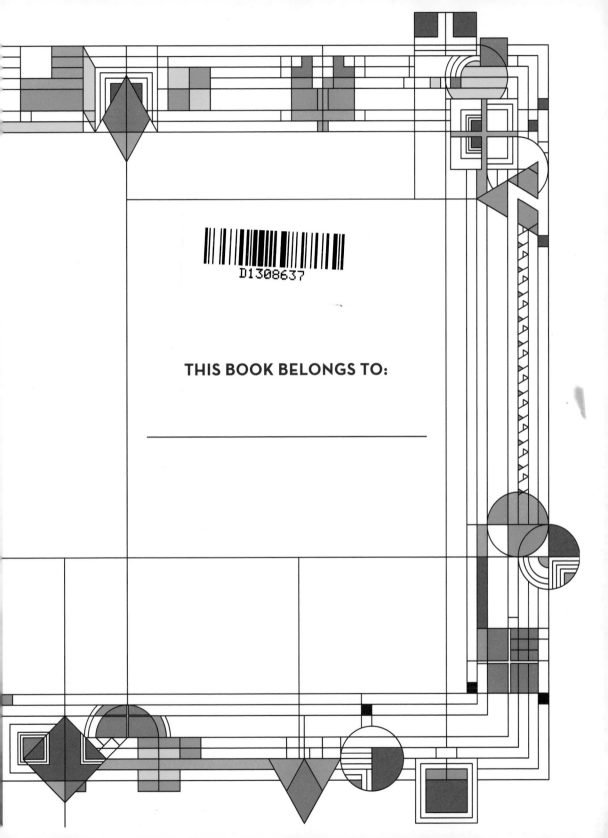

THIS BOOK BELONGS TO:

_____

FRANK LLOYD WRIGHT (1867-1959)

became a very important American architect who created over one thousand buildings like houses, churches, museums, and colleges.

Mr. Wright was not only a talented architect, he also enjoyed making drawings and designs of art glass, furniture, dinnerware, rugs, and many other decorative items for his buildings.

When Wright was a child, his mother gave him a gift of spheres, cubes, triangles, rectangular and triangular prisms, classic building blocks, and paper. His exploratory play with these basic geometric shapes and observations of patterns in nature as a child developed into a unique architectural and graphic design style.

When Frank Lloyd Wright was a boy, he was given a set of educational toys called the Froebel Gifts and Occupations by his mother, Anna. Anna Lloyd Wright, a teacher herself, bought these toys for her family at an exhibition in Philadelphia, and Wright spent much time playing with the blocks during his childhood years.

Cut out these shapes!

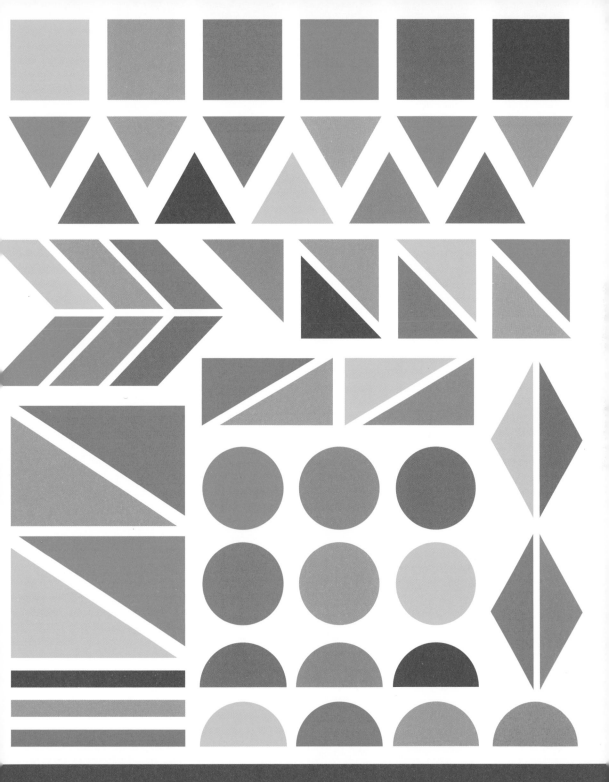

Cut out these shapes!

These are some examples of designs you can create with the cutout shapes.

Frank Lloyd Wright used materials appropriate to the environment surrounding the structure. He used wood for houses built in forests and stone for houses built in the desert.

📍 **NORMAN LYKES HOUSE** is located in Phoenix, Arizona

📍 The **HERBERT AND KATHERINE JACOBS I HOUSE** is located in Madison, Wisconsin

What is your favorite environment? What kind of house would you build there? Think of materials that would be appropriate for the environment.

Draw a house in your favorite environment.

Frank Lloyd Wright designed this dinnerware set for the dining room of the Imperial Hotel in Tokyo, Japan. He unified the designs of these round plates, cups, saucers, and bowls by using just circles in his compositions.

Design your own dinnerware set for your kitchen.

Look at the Hoffman House Rug design. Where did Mr. Wright use color?
Where did he leave white space?

Color your own Hoffman Rug!

This is the architectural floor plan of the Arthur Heurtley House.

An architectural floor plan lays out the entire design of the house or building. It shows how you enter the house, where the rooms are, indicates windows and doors, and it often shows where the furniture will be.

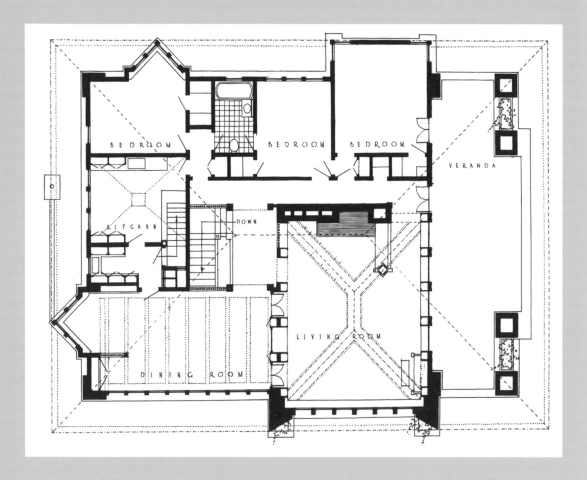

ARTHUR HEURTLEY HOUSE is located in Oak Park, Illinois

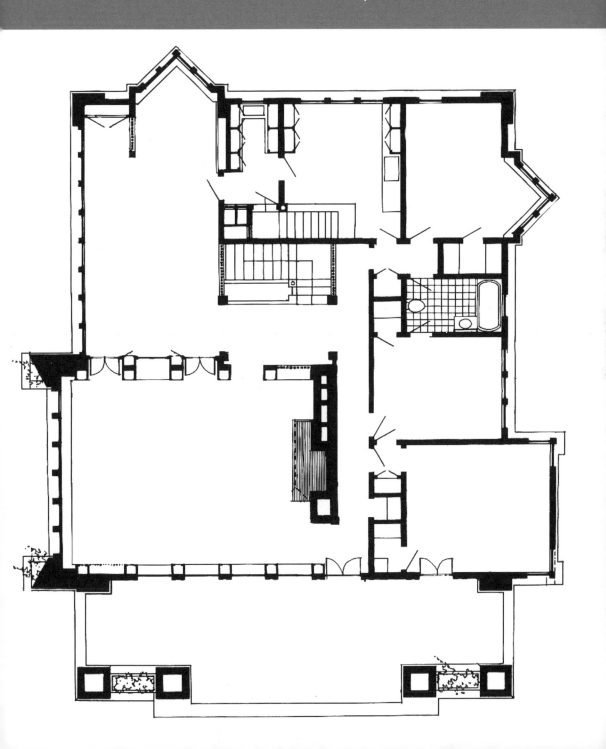

This abstract design by Mr. Wright is called May Basket. It depicts a basket of overflowing fruit in springtime.

Color your own May Basket!

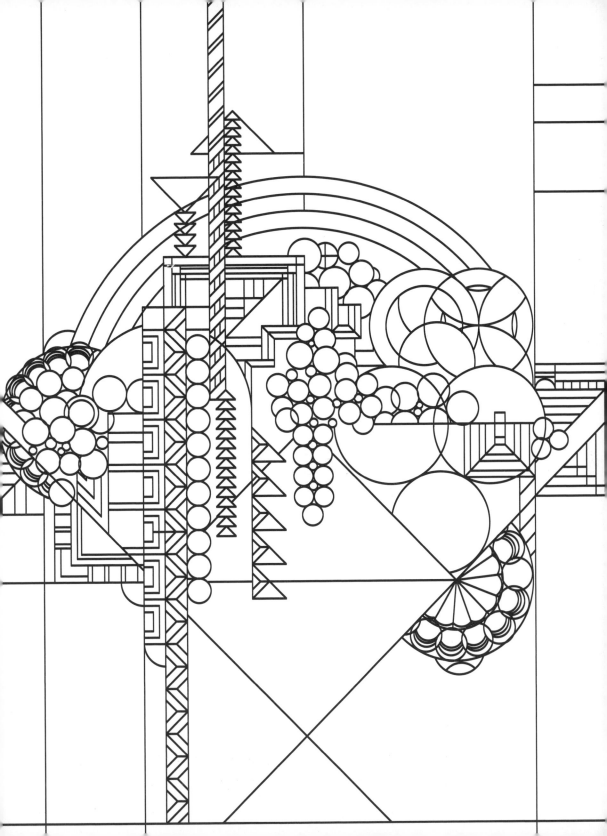

Clients play an important role in an architect's work. They tell the architect their ideas and wishes for the building. The architect listens to them and then uses his/her own vision to design the right building.

Friend's name:

_____

House wish list:

_____

_____

_____

_____

Interview a friend and write down 4 wishes he/she would have for his/her dream house.

Draw a house for your friend!

Consider your friend's wishes for the house. How can you successfully incorporate his/her requests? Show him/her your final drawing!

This California Textile Block House has block patterns arranged across its exterior and interior walls. This patterned surface gives the house a unique texture.

  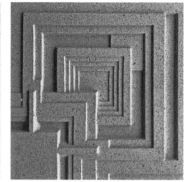

This block pattern is used 27,000 times throughout the house!

📍 The **ENNIS HOUSE** is located in Los Angeles, California

Create your own block pattern here

Now, using the grid as a guide, repeat the pattern you created on the exterior of this house.

In the mural "City By The Sea," Frank Lloyd Wright created the feeling of the Chicago skyline with balloons, confetti, and vibrant colors that he must have seen when his career began there in 1887.

This mural was designed in 1913 for the entertainment complex, Midway Gardens, and perished when it was torn down. In 1957, the mural design was revived for the Music Pavilion at Taliesin West in Scottsdale, Arizona.

What landscape would you put in your mural?
Draw it using only geometric shapes.

The Price Tower is the only skyscraper designed by Mr. Wright that was actually built. He called it "the tree that escaped the crowded forest."

📍 The **PRICE TOWER** is located in Bartlesville, Oklahoma

Create your own festive window design below!

Frank Lloyd Wright was inspired by butterflies when he designed these windows for the Dana-Thomas House. Can you see the resemblance?

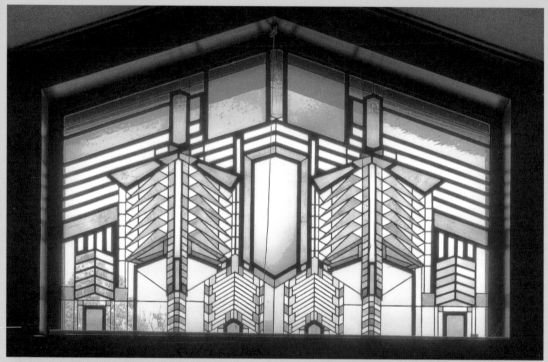

📍 **DANA-THOMAS HOUSE** is located in Springfield, Illinois

Create a bug inspired pattern!

Use only geometric shapes. For a simpler pattern, use less shapes.
For a more detailed pattern, use more shapes.

Architects draw their building designs from 4 different viewpoints. They draw these viewpoints so that the client or the builder can have a better understanding of what it will look like or how to build it.

These are examples of each viewpoint drawing for one of Frank Lloyd Wright's most famous buildings, Fallingwater.

FLOOR PLAN (bird's-eye view)

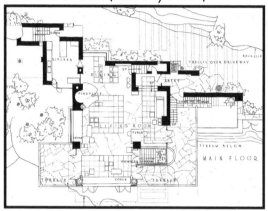

ELEVATION (view from the side)

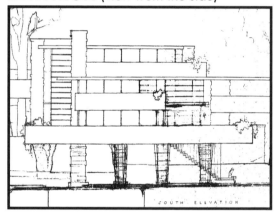

SECTION (view from a cut)

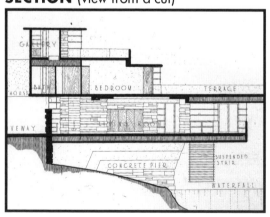

PERSPECTIVE (view at an angle)

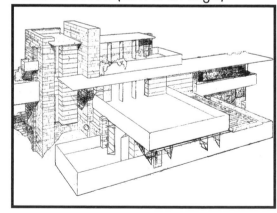

♀ FALLINGWATER is located in Mill Run, Pennsylvania

Now it's your turn! Using the opposite page as reference, draw an apple from the 4 viewpoints.

FLOOR PLAN (bird's-eye view)

ELEVATION (view from the side)

SECTION (view from a cut)

PERSPECTIVE (view at an angle)

Ask an adult to help cut the apple in half.

Frank Lloyd Wright said, "Every chair must be designed for the building it is to be used in." Mr. Wright designed the chairs below specifically for each building's interior. Observe the chairs and the environment they were intended for. What similarities do you see?

The Barrel Chair was designed for the Herbert F. Johnson House (Wingspread).

📍 **WINGSPREAD** is located in Wind Point, Wisconsin

The Origami Chair was designed for Taliesin West.

📍 **TALIESIN WEST** is located in Scottsdale, Arizona

The Johnson Wax Chair was designed for the S.C. Johnson Administration Building.

📍 **S.C. JOHNSON ADMINISTRATION BUILDING** is located in Racine, Wisconsin

Design a chair for your favorite room!

This stained glass window, called "Tree of Life," was designed by Mr. Wright for the Darwin D. Martin House. He was inspired by the natural landscape surrounding the area.

How would you color the trees on the next page?

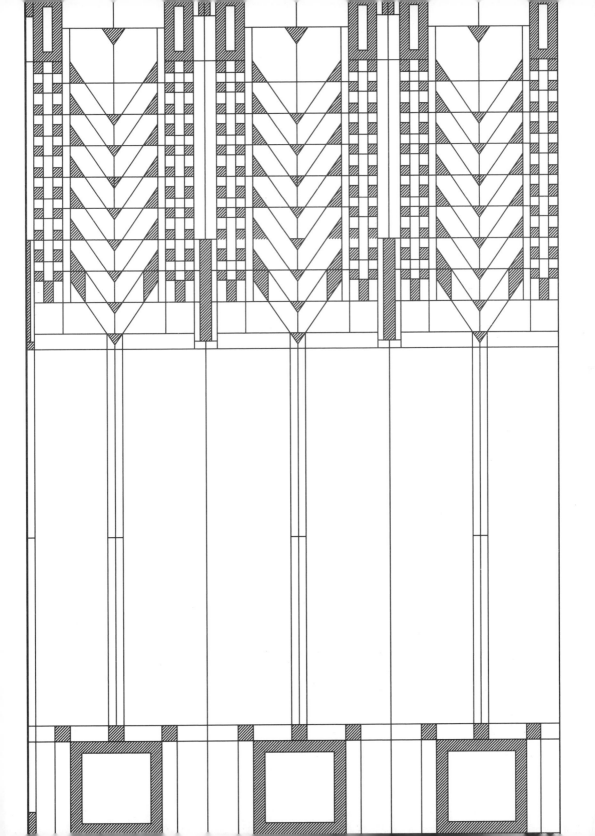

Frank Lloyd Wright loved imagining what the future would look like.
He designed the futuristic Annunciation Greek Orthodox Church in the 1950s.

📍 **ANNUNCIATION GREEK ORTHODOX CHURCH** is located in Wauwatosa, Wisconsin

Draw a futuristic building.

Imagine what buildings will look like in 50 years.

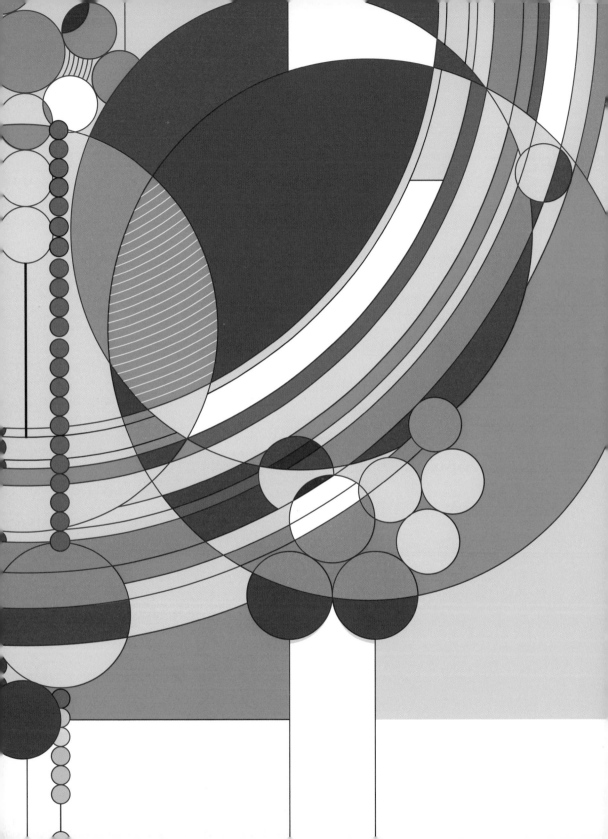

This is Frank Lloyd Wright's "March Balloons" design. He used only circles to create this composition. Notice his use of scale, repetition, and white space.

Create your own design with the repetition of 1 shape in various sizes.

Frank Lloyd Wright traveled to Japan and fell in love with the culture. He was inspired by Japanese pagodas like the one below when he designed Wingspread on the opposite page.

What do these 2 buildings have in common?

⊙ WINGSPREAD is located in Wind Point, Wisconsin

When designing a space, architects consider how people's senses react to everything they see, hear, smell, and feel. This exercise will help you analyze your experiences every time you step into a new place.

Go to your favorite room and fill up this chart

WHAT DO YOU FEEL?

What surfaces & textures do you feel in the space?

_____

_____

_____

What temperatures can you identify? Hot/cold?

_____

_____

_____

What do you feel? Why do you think this space makes you feel this way?

_____

_____

_____

WHAT DO YOU SEE?

How big is the space? Can you see its entire shape?

_____

_____

_____

What are the colors used in the space? Are they dark or light?

_____

_____

_____

Describe the light. Where is the light coming from?

_____

_____

_____

 **WHAT DO YOU HEAR?**

Talk loudly. Do you hear an echo?

_____
_____
_____

Close your eyes. Describe what you hear.

_____
_____
_____

Can you hear the outside world? What about noise from the other rooms?

_____
_____
_____

 **WHAT DO YOU SMELL?**

Can you describe what scents are present?

_____
_____
_____

Are there good or bad smells in this space?

_____
_____
_____

Does the smell in this space remind you of anything?

_____
_____
_____

Abstraction is an art technique where you simplify a subject's form down to its essential characteristics.

Frank Lloyd Wright was inspired by hollyhock flowers when he created this decoration for the exterior of the Hollyhock House. See his abstraction process below!

Nature inspiration

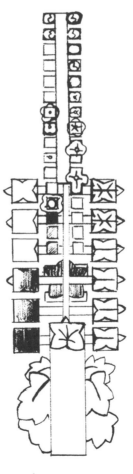

In progress

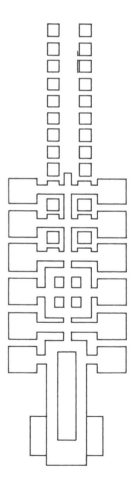

Final abstraction

Create your own nature abstraction!

Use this photo of lilies as an inspiration to practice abstraction in the spaces below.

Nature inspiration

In progress

Final abstraction

Mr. Wright designed this pattern with the Fourth of July celebration in mind.
Do you see all the American flags?

Color the opposite page!

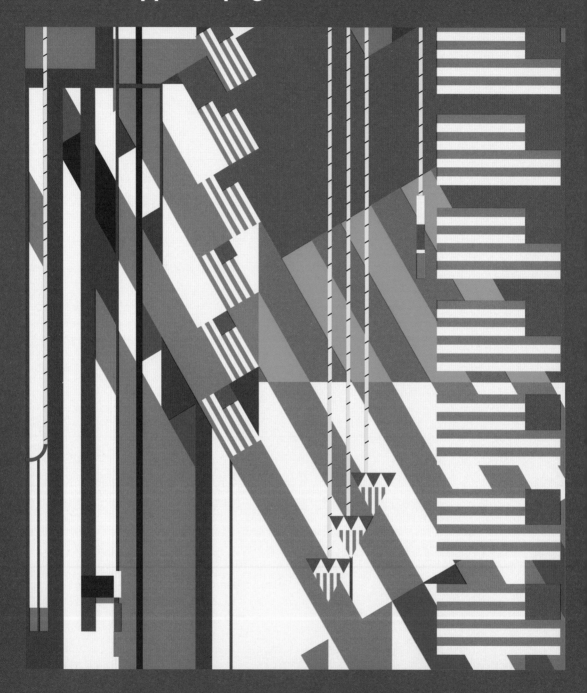

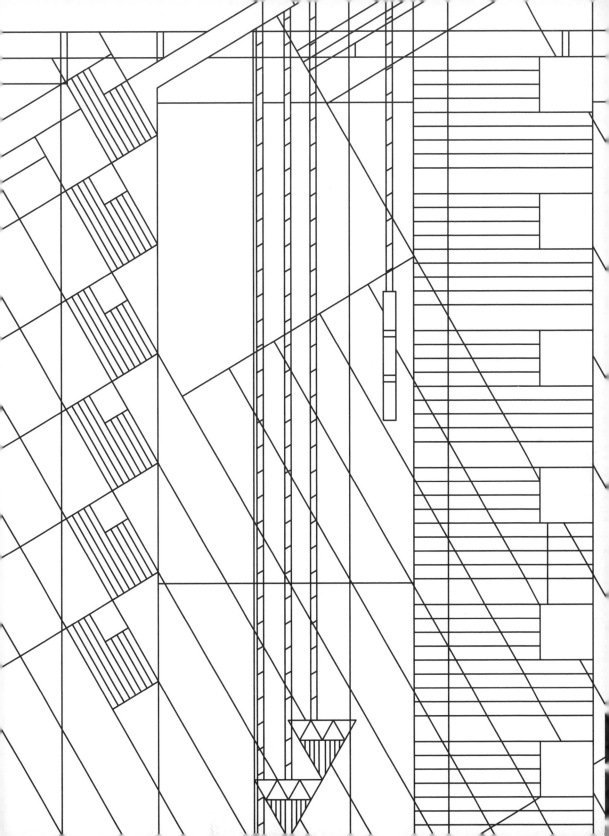

Below is the floor plan Frank Lloyd Wright drafted for the Vigo Sundt House. This house is designed using hexagons to create a pattern.

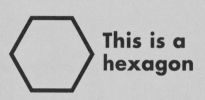 **This is a hexagon**

 **This is a hexagonal pattern**

Look for the hexagonal pattern in this floor plan.

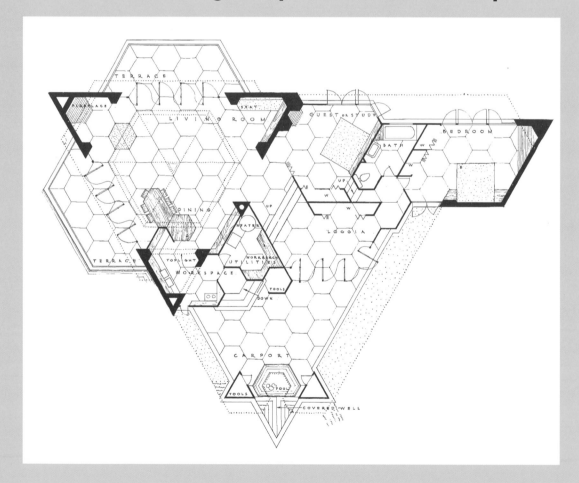

⚲ VIGO SUNDT HOUSE was designed for a site in Madison, Wisconsin

Create a pattern by repeating geometric shapes.

Use the grid below to create a design for a blanket.

In 1956, a 12 year old boy wrote to Frank Lloyd Wright asking him to build a dog house to keep his dog warm during the winter. Frank Lloyd Wright fulfilled the boy's request.

June 19, 1956

Dear Mr. Wright,

I am a boy of twelve years. My name is Jim Berger. You designed a house for my father whose name is Bob Berger. I have a paper route which I make a little bit of money for the bank, and for expenses.

I would appreciate it if you would design me a dog house, which would be easy to build, but would go with our house. My dog's name is Edward, but we call him Eddie. He is 4 years old or in dog life 28 years. He is a Labrador retriever. He is two and a half feet high and three feet long. The reasons I would like this dog house is for the winters mainly. My dad said if you design the dog house he will help me build it. But if you design the dog house I will pay you for the plans and materials out of the money I get from my route.

Respectfully yours,
Jim Berger

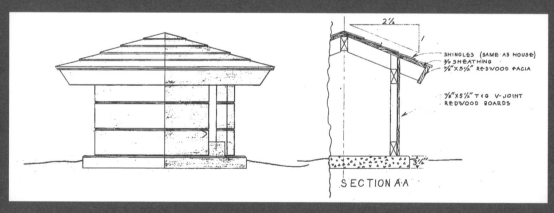

SECTION A·A

2½"

SHINGLES (SAME AS HOUSE)
¾ SHEATHING
⅞"×5½" REDWOOD FACIA

⅞"×5½" T&G V-JOINT REDWOOD BOARDS

EDDIE'S DOG HOUSE was located in San Anselmo, California

Draw a house for a pet, real or imaginary.

What materials would you use? How big would it be?

The Guggenheim Museum in New York City has been compared to an inverted cupcake, a washing machine, and a giant Jell-O mold, but Wright was actually inspired by a seashell.

📍 The **SOLOMON R. GUGGENHEIM MUSEUM** is located in New York City, New York

Draw a building with an unexpected shape.

How will it look from above? What is the building's purpose?
Will your final design surprise people?

Frank Lloyd Wright was inspired by a cactus when he created this design.
Can you see the similarities between the two images below?

Draw your own abstraction of a cactus.

Use only geometric shapes. What shapes will you use?
How will you use color and repetition?

Wright designed over 1,000 buildings in many different forms and shapes. He designed churches, small and large homes, civic buildings, schools, and museums. He also designed bridges, skyscrapers, and hotels. Less than half of all of his designs have been built.

Complete the other sides of these buildings. What will they look like?

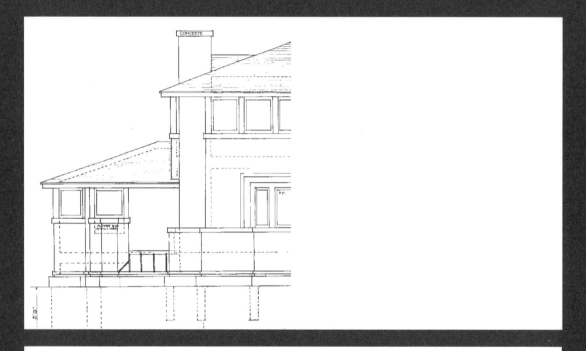

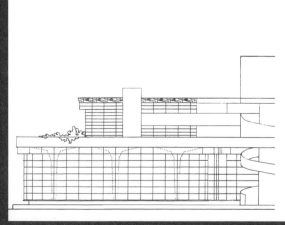

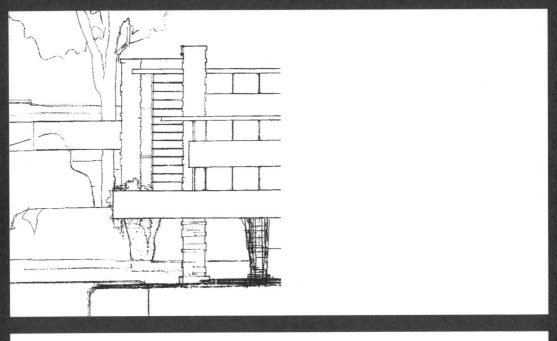

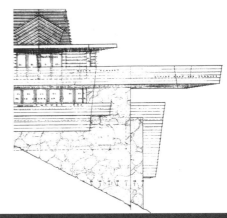

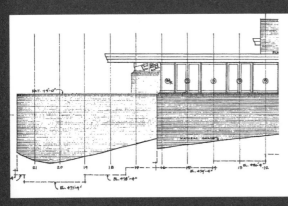

Mr. Wright designed this rug for the Imperial Hotel in Japan.

Mr. Wright was fascinated with the automobile and he designed many cars and other vehicles. Below is an example of one of his car designs.

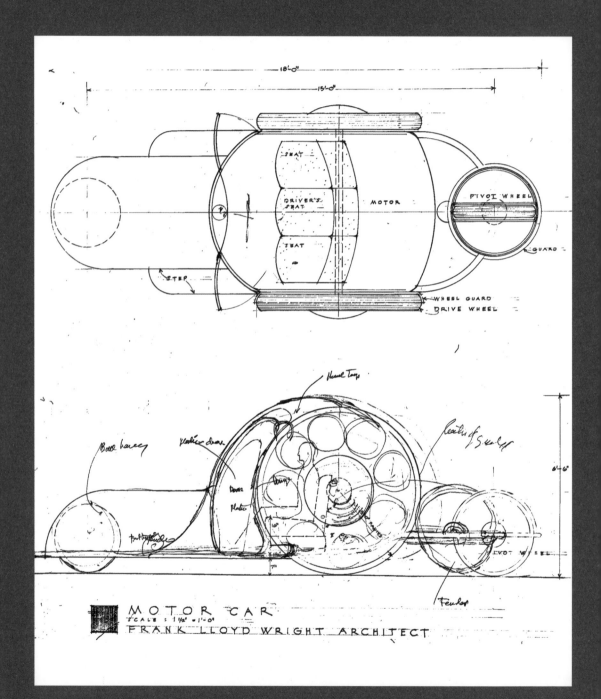

Draw a futuristic car!

What kind of vehicle will you design? How many windows and wheels will it have? What energy will power your futuristic car?

Credits

♀ Continue your architectural experience by visiting a Frank Lloyd Wright site near you!

There are more than 70 Frank Lloyd Wright buildings open to the public.
Visit www.franklloydwright.org to plan your next architectural adventure.